True Tails II from the Dog Park
By Max and Luther

Illustrations by Julie Ann Stricklin

Visit our website: www.kariandcarey.com
Facebook: maxandlutherpublication
Instagram: maxandluther
Twitter: @dogparktails

Purchase our book:
www.maxandluther.com
www.amazon.com
www.barnesandnoble.com
Also available at fine independent bookstores everywhere

First published by Dog Ear Publishing
4011 Vincennes Rd
Indianapolis, IN 46268
www.dogearpublishing.net

ISBN: 978-1-4575-4055-4

Library of Congress Control Number: has been applied for

This book is printed on acid-free paper.

Printed in the United States of America

Dedication:

"Be the person your dog thinks you are." – Unknown

About the Authors

Max Sherman- Max is a three-year-old Puggle (half-Beagle, half-Pug) with an all-Beagle personality. Max loves food and can smell crumbs in your pocket from last week. Because he is so curious, Max is also a world-class thief. If you meet him, hang on to your purse or bag! This dog loves all people and dogs so he always enjoys going to new places to make new friends. Max has a lot of energy, and can often be seen walking in the neighborhood or playing in the dog park. I am never afraid he will get lost, as everyone knows him. Max loves getting his picture taken with his fans, and sometimes gets jealous when Luther gets more attention than he does. – **Co-author Kari Sherman**

Luther Laubenberg ("Lou") - Luther is a two-year-old Olde English Bulldog. As there are not many of these dogs around, Luther always gets a lot of attention, mostly because he is so big! I like to think of him as a train—slow to get going, and even slower to stop. While Luther is a big boy, he is also the sweetest and gentlest of dogs. He really loves all the little dogs and puppies at the park. He will lie down, legs sprawled out behind him, and let the little ones jump all over him, pull on his jowls, and nip at his bum. He never gets tired of it. Luther has a very unique way of walking—his stomach goes one direction, and his bum and head go the other way. I call it his swagger. You cannot help stopping to look at him when he walks down the street. Most people have never seen such a big and handsome Bulldog before! - **Co-author Carey Laubenberg**

Chapter 1

Fun Facts

🐾 Dogs sweat through their paws.

🐾 A dog uses eighteen muscles to move its ear.

🐾 Nose prints are used to identify dogs just like a fingerprint.

🐾 Dogs have a wet nose to help them get smells from the air and ground.

🐾 Dalmatians are born all white without any spots.

🐾 Chow Chows are born with pink tongues, which change to a blue-black color as they get older.

🐾 Dogs can be either left or right handed (pawed).

🐾 A dog's shoulder blades move independently from the rest of the skeleton to allow greater flexibility for running.

Mud Buffet!

I cannot explain it, but there is something so awesome about the mud at the dog park after a good rain. Not everyone knows that it rarely rains in Southern California, so there are not many chances for me to enjoy my "mud buffet"! Let me explain what I mean by "mud buffet." Instead of being one of those dogs that likes to roll in the mud, I prefer to eat it! I shovel it in by the mouthful (a very large mouthful). I go about my mud-eating madness in a very specific way. As my pal Max enjoys hunting gophers, I follow him around the dog park on his quest. Max will spot a gopher hole and go to check it out. Sometimes he has to dig a little in order to reach the gopher, and when he fails to get to the gopher (as he always does), he moves on to the next gopher hole. This is when I spring into action! I swoop in and begin shoveling the mud into my mouth. Mouthful by mouthful, the gopher hole gets deeper and deeper while I get dirtier and dirtier. The way I see it, I am being a good friend to Max by helping him get closer to the gophers.

My mom calls me a Bulldog mud machine and she does NOT like it when I eat mud. Mom is forever pulling me out of the mud holes, but I always find another one quickly. She even tries to stand guard over the hole to stop me from reaching my latest meal! Well, let's just say that this does not stop me at all. I still try to eat as much mud as possible because, let's face it; I never know when it will rain again. Maybe I should move to Seattle!!!! – **Luther**

No Control Remote Control

I have this "friend" who can be very mischievous, and one day he was wandering through the house looking for something to do. Suddenly, he saw something interesting in the bedroom. He slowly entered the room to check it out. On the bed there was this amazing white bone-like object with black spots! *Perfect,* he thought, *a new toy to play with.* This "friend" jumped on the bed and began to happily chew away at his new toy. Meanwhile, in the other room, his parents were quietly watching TV, unaware of the mischief in the other room. Suddenly, they realized that they had not seen or heard my "friend" in quite a while. The parents went in search of their mischievous puppy and found, to their surprise, that he was halfway through eating the remote control!!!! Not good; not good at all. Now, you may have guessed that my "friend" was really me! The moral of this story is that when you cannot see or hear your dog, you can bet that nothing good is happening. You always need a watchful eye on us so we don't get into trouble. -**"Friend" of Luther**

Top Ten Jobs for Dogs

Chapter 2

Fun Facts

- The Basenji sheds little to no hair, and washes itself like a cat.

  - The hair of a Komondor must never be combed or brushed. It is divided into cords and trimmed.

- There are no completely hypoallergenic dogs.

  - Dogs curl up in a ball when they sleep due to an instinct to keep themselves warm and protect their tummies.

- The oldest officially recorded age of a dog is 29 years 5 months.

  - The poodle haircut was originally meant to improve the dog's swimming abilities as a retriever, with the pom-poms left in place to warm their legs.

- Sled Dogs burn an average of 10,000 calories per day during a sled race.

Teddy Bear Tug-O-War

It was my first day at the dog beach and it was wonderful. The sun was out, there were tons of dogs to play with, and I was a very happy Olde English Bulldog. While I was walking around the beach checking things out, I noticed a teddy bear. His arms were out as if to say, "Come get me", so I did! I couldn't believe it. My first day at dog beach and someone brought me a teddy bear! As I began to walk away with Ted (his new name), I noticed something pulling him in the other direction. All of a sudden I was having a tug-o-war with someone. I looked up and saw a mother holding hands with her child who was wearing Ted as a backpack!! The mother was heading in one direction, while I was heading in the other direction, with the kid and Ted dangling in the middle! I saw the instant the mother realized that a stuffed bear attached to a small child at the dog beach was not a good idea. Ted the backpack came off the child very quickly while my mom scolded me about taking the toy. Neither the kid nor I were very happy about that but Ted lived to see another day! –**Luther**

Rattlesnake Roundup

I live in Southern California, and that means there are all sorts of other animals besides us dogs around (which is quite enough, thank you!!). But there are mainly coyotes and rattlesnakes. I want to tell you about my encounter with a rattlesnake. It all started one day at the local dog park. I was happily playing with all my friends and Mom was chatting away (as usual) with her group of humans. Suddenly, this man cried out in fear! Everybody turned and looked his way. There in the middle of the dog park, unconcerned with both dog and human alike, was a rattlesnake, slithering along! All the dogs and humans ran away in fear. Not me! I was curious because I had never seen a rattlesnake before, so I went over to check it out. Mom was yelling my name, but I was too busy to pay attention. This thing was something new and different.

Just when I was about to sniff the snake (yes, I was that close!), Mom threw her sunglasses at me and hit my nose! Was that really necessary? Well of course that did the trick and I backed away from the snake, but I was pretty mad at Mom. I ran away from her and her friends as they tried to capture me. *Hey!* I thought to myself, *this is a fun game of chase!* Finally, they cornered me and I was taken back to the car. I didn't understand what the big deal was. I am always curious about everything, and never had sunglasses thrown at me before. The next weekend I found myself at a rattlesnake avoidance class. Yes, there is actually such a class for dogs. That was the most unpleasant experience of my whole life, but you'd better believe that I will NEVER approach a rattlesnake ever again. – **Max**

Max and Luther's Top Ten Books about Dogs

1. **Where the Red Fern Grows** *Wilson Rawls*
2. **The Incredible Journey** Sheila Burnford
3. **White Fang/Call of the Wild** *Jack London*
4. **Rin Tin Tin** *Susan Orlean*
5. **Old Yeller** *Frank Gipson*
6. **Lassie Come Home** *Eric Knight*
7. **Marley and Me** *John Grogan*
8. **A Dog's Purpose** *W. Bruce Cameron*
9. **The Art of Racing in the Rain** *Garth Stein*
10. **Chet and Bernie Series** *Spencer Quinn*
11. **True Tails from the Dog Park** *Max and Luther*

Fun Facts

All dogs are descendants of wolves.

There are more than 700 different breeds of dogs.

In total, there are around 400 million dogs in the world.

More money is spent each year on dog food than baby food.

The normal body temperature for a dog is 101.2 degrees Fahrenheit.

It costs about $10,000 to train a search and rescue dog.

Mixed breed dogs or "mutts" are called "All-American" dogs.

Thirty percent of American families own a dog.

On average, dogs understand 200 words.

Is this Normal?

Every dog has a personality, right? We are just like humans; some of us are smart, shy, lazy, social, stubborn, happy, or sad, etc. The point is, every one of us dogs is different. Who's to say what is normal or not? Isn't variety the spice of life? Mom often talks to other humans about what she calls my "quirky" behaviors. I don't understand it; this is just the way I am!

One of my quirky behaviors that Mom can't understand is that sometimes when I am given a treat or a rawhide chew I like to bark at it, then play with it before I eat it. Mom always bursts out laughing and tells me to just eat it! I love getting treats (I am part Beagle, after all!), but sometimes I am just so happy to get it that I can't help myself. So I bark for joy and then wrestle with it and toss it around. It's fun! I can't explain it; why should I have to?

Another odd thing I do that always confuses my mom is that when I am at the beach or the dog park, I like to dig a hole then run circles around it. Something about digging that hole gets me excited and I can't help but to run around like a crazy dog! I also really like when there is another dog around because it ends up in a super-fun game of chase. One of my favorite games is being chased by another dog. I am pretty fast, and can change directions quickly. Only another really fast dog like a Greyhound can keep up. Not bad for a Puggle, if I do say so myself! - **Max**

Dogs in Diapers

I have two friends at the dog park whose names I will leave to your imagination, as they wear diapers. Yes, I did say diapers! They call them "pants," but they are actually just diapers. The dogs do not have to wear them at the park, but they do wear them pretty much everywhere else. Why do they have to wear them? you ask. Well, these dogs wear diapers because they are naughty. They like to pee on everything, which is also known as "marking their territory." Of course, these dogs like to mark everybody else's territory too, not just their own. It is amazing how much these two dogs can pee!

The funny part of this story is that often when the boys are out on their "potty" walk; their parents forget to take off their pants. The dogs are actually peeing in their pants! And to make matters worse, the diapers are always very colorful, so everyone—dogs and humans alike—notice them. How embarrassing!!! As you can imagine, the dogs were very upset with their humans for forgetting to remove their pants in public. They haven't shown up at the dog park in their diapers yet, but it is sure to happen one day. I hope I am there to see that! I promise I won't laugh—at least not out loud. -**Luther**

Top Ten Dog Breeds in the U. S.

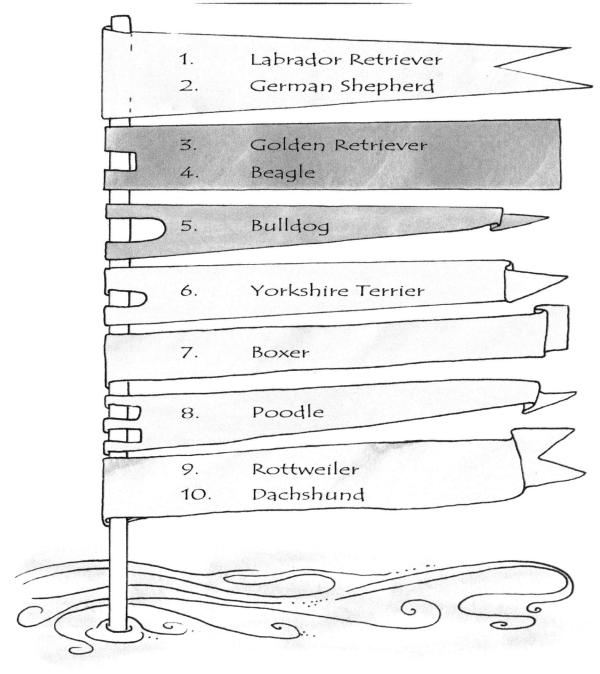

1. Labrador Retriever
2. German Shepherd
3. Golden Retriever
4. Beagle
5. Bulldog
6. Yorkshire Terrier
7. Boxer
8. Poodle
9. Rottweiler
10. Dachshund

Chapter 4

Fun Facts

- Small dogs tend to live longer than big dogs.

- The largest recorded dog was Zorba, an English Mastiff, who weighed 343 pounds and was 8 feet 3 inches tall.

- The smartest dog is believed to be the Border Collie.

- The Afghan Hound is thought to be one of the least intelligent dogs.

- The smallest dog was a Yorkshire Terrier that weighed only four ounces and was two and a half inches tall.

- The first animal to orbit the earth was a Russian dog named Laika, in 1957.

- The dog name Fido means "fidelity" in Latin.

- There have been more than 50 dogs that have lived in the White House.

- President Lyndon Johnson had two Beagles named Him and Her.

Fun Games

I don't know about other dogs, but sometimes I get bored. Humans assume that if we dogs get daily walks or trips to the dog park/beach, we should be happy. Well, I am here to tell you that just like you humans, dogs become bored doing the same thing every day. I need a variety of activities to keep me happy and healthy. Lucky for me, Mom gets that fact. She has come up with a number of games to keep me interested. Now, these games may seem simple to you but I love them! I thought I would share some of my favorite games with you.

One of my favorite games in the house is hide and seek. My mom will have me sit and stay and then she hides somewhere in the house so I have to find her. Well, I am here to tell you that I rock at this game! I always find her hiding place. This game is perfect for a rainy day or a too-hot-for-both-human-and-dog day! Another game I love is attack the broom! Now, I am not actually sure if my mom thinks this is a game, but I do. When Mom tries to sweep the patio, or even the kitchen floor, it is on! I love trying to get the broom in my mouth. Mom lifts the broom high in the air and twirls it about but I am always after it, and I can jump pretty high! The only bad part of this game is that it always ends in the same way: I am shut up in another room while she finishes sweeping. She does seem to go along with the game for a little while before this happens.

When we are in a park running around off-leash, one of my favorite games is to try to catch the leash. Mom will trail the leash after her and when I try to get it, up in the air it goes. I love to run and jump up after the leash. I am a great jumper! Now, my leash does not necessarily taste that good, but I am attracted to the herky-jerky motion and cannot help trying to get it. I think Mom likes this game too because it always seems to make her laugh (I secretly think she is in awe of my jumping ability!). Another great game is tug-o-war. Naturally, I have put my own spin on it. Instead of just trying to get the rope from Mom, I actually want her to pull me around the house with the rope in my mouth. I think this is super-fun, and if Mom isn't pulling me fast enough, I untuck my paw and use it like an oar to go faster! Everyone always laughs at this game – humans are weird!

Last but not least is the game I like to call "Hide the Nub." Now, for those who don't know what a nub is, it is the leftover part of a rawhide bone (usually the knotted end) that I do not finish chewing. I like to gather these nubs and then hide them all around the house. When one of my friends comes to visit, I head directly to one of my hiding places so they can't have it and I can tease them with it! Every once in a while I catch Mom taking the hidden bones and throwing them away. I don't know why she does that; they are still perfectly good chews! - **Max**

SoCal Dog

Living in Southern California is great. I live a mile from a dog beach, which we visit quite often from the fall to the spring. Summer, however, is another matter. Del Mar is a beach town, and every summer we get flooded with tourists. They come to enjoy our beaches, go to the San Diego Fair or the Del Mar Race Track. With so many tourists coming into our town in the summer, our local dog beach made some "summer rules." Basically what that means is NO off-leash fun at the beach. I do not like that rule because I LOVE the beach. Mom actually doesn't mind the summer rules because with so many people at the beach, I tend to get into trouble. Did I happen to tell you that I am a world-class thief? Well, it's true—any food or open bag is very interesting to me.

Another great thing about Southern California is the weather. It is usually sunny and 70 degrees much of the year; however, it does rain in the winter. Man, I hate the rain. I get all wet, muddy, and stinky, which of course means a bath. I do not like taking a bath! I don't squirm or fuss but I do give Mom this very sad look. Mom does not like stinky dogs because I sleep in her bed every night (I love to snuggle). Anyway, back to the weather. I do not like it when it is either too hot or too cold—kind of like Goldilocks. Sometimes when I am naughty, Mom threatens to take me on a trip to visit her family in Ohio where it SNOWS! Now, I have never seen snow, but I KNOW I would not like it. So at least for now I am going to behave. – **Max**

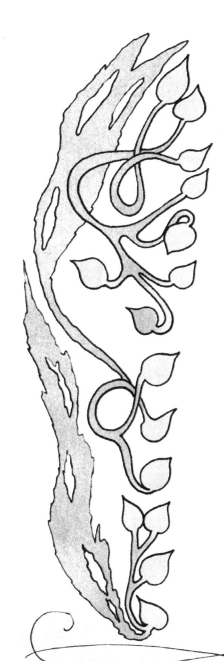

Max and Luther's Top Movies about Dogs

1. Hachi: A Dog's Tale

2. Lady and the Tramp

3. Homeward Bound: An Incredible Journey

4. Old Yeller

5. Beethoven

6. Marley and Me

7. Where the Red Fern Grows

8. Benji

9. Eight Below

10. The Fox and the Hound

11. 101 Dalmatians

12. Milo and Otis

Chapter 5

Fun Facts

🐾 Dogs' eyes are special and they can see in the dark.

🐾 Dogs can also see in color, but not as many colors as humans can.

🐾 A puppy is born blind, deaf, and toothless.

🐾 Dogs have three eyelids: an upper lid, a lower lid, and the third lid, which helps to keep the eye moist and protected.

🐾 A dog's whiskers are touch-sensitive hairs that actually sense small changes in the air around them.

🐾 Not all Rhodesian Ridgebacks have ridges.

🐾 The Mexican hairless dogs have great body heat, which makes them great bed warmers.

Two Toads

Scamper was a dog who liked to get into trouble, and was always getting into things he should not have. One of Scamper's favorite activities was watching his dad plant new vegetables in the garden. As soon as Dad turned his back, Scamper would dig up all the plants. His dad would get mad and chase him around the yard with the garden hose, trying to get him with the water, but he was really just hoping to rinse some of the dirt off Scamper. This was an activity that they would do almost every week. What is really funny is that Scamper's dad could have just closed the gate and locked him out of the garden. I think that he enjoyed their game as much as Scamper did!

One day, their game of chase was cut short when Scamper discovered a toad. He thought it looked more interesting than the plants and decided to have a taste. Bad idea! Toads have a poison in their skin that is dangerous, and can really hurt a dog if it is not treated right away. Scamper's dad quickly put down the hose when he noticed that the dog was in pain, and rushed him to the vet. Scamper was treated by the vet and was fine. His bad behavior was forgotten for about a week. That is about how long it took him to get better, get back into the garden, and find another toad!! Yes, that is right, he found another toad. Two toads in two weeks—it was a record! Scamper was not a smart dog, and had not learned from his mistake. After the second trip to the vet, Scamper's dad got smart and started to leave him inside the house when he was in the garden. I think that Scamper secretly missed playing with the garden hose, but there were no more trips to the vet due to the toads. – **Luther**

25

The Escape Artist

My mom had a number of different dogs when she was growing up (although none were as great as me!). One of my favorite stories is that of her dog Buzzy, a very silly mutt. Of course, these days you would call him an All-American dog. Buzzy was very well-known in his neighborhood. He frequently escaped the backyard and ran down the block to the public pool. Naturally, he managed to wiggle his way into the pool area and join the kids for a fun swim. At least twice a week, Grandpa would get a call from the lifeguards at the pool asking him to come and get his dog. These adventures made Buzzy very popular with the kids in the neighborhood, but not so much with their parents or the lifeguards.

These daring escapes eventually led to Buzzy being tied to a long leash when he was in the backyard unsupervised. Thus begins part two of the story… Buzzy was a very determined dog and wanted to run free. So Buzzy started jumping the fence (while still on the leash), which always got him stuck on the other side of the fence! Mom's family thought that after he did this once, that would be the end of it. Unfortunately, Buzzy was not the smartest of dogs…he did it over and over again, until it became quite the joke. Finally, the family found the perfect spot in the yard where Buzzy could not reach the fence anymore and his adventures were over. It just goes to show you that dogs can be very determined, even when they are not very smart! – **Max**

Top Ten Dog Names

1. Bella
2. Max
3. Buddy
4. Lucy
5. Daisy
6. Molly
7. Bailey
8. Maggie
9. Charlie
10. Sadie

Chapter 6

Fun Facts

- A dog's sense of smell is 10,000 to 100,000 times better than a human's.

- Dogs have less than a fifth of the taste buds of humans.

- A one-year-old dog is equal to a 15-year-old teenager.

- Dogs hear sounds up to four times farther away than humans do.

- The Greyhound is the fastest dog and can run up to 45 mph.

- The Saluki is one of the oldest breeds of dogs.

- The Beagle and Collie are the nosiest dogs.

- The Basenji is the quietest, as they do not bark.

The Hunt Begins

I have a confession. I love hunting gophers! I don't care about bunnies, birds, lizards—and I am afraid of cats—but I love gophers. At one of my favorite local dog parks, there are tons of gophers. I am obsessed with them! I go from hole to hole in search of them. Those gophers are so annoying! Sometimes they peek up out of the hole to check out what is going on. They are so bold; I think that they are doing this just to annoy me. I will stand and stare intently at the hole for a long time waiting for those gophers to appear. I often turn my head slowly from one side to the other trying to hear them. My mom thinks I look like a pointer because I lift my right leg and point my head towards the hole while I am waiting for the gopher to appear. Then suddenly, I hear and smell the little guy coming. I crouch to gather myself for the spring, and then I am in the air. My whole body flings towards the hole and my head disappears down it. Rats! I missed again. I have not caught one yet, but I am going to keep on trying. I think my mom is secretly happy that I have not caught one yet, but I know she thinks it is funny watching me try. Sometimes it is hard work keeping her laughing, but that is part of my job. Watch out, gophers, I am coming for you! - **Max**

Second Place by a Lick!

One day, Mom decided to sign me up for a peanut butter eating contest since, as she puts it, I am "chow hound." I can eat my dinner in five seconds flat! For the contest, they put us dogs into small and large groups. Somehow that meant I ended up in the small dog group. I was very sure that I would win first place. I know that Mom was eyeing the gift basket as if it was a done deal.

I watched the large dog round with interest as my buddy, Luther, was competing in that group. Luther was pretty funny, as most of the peanut butter went around his mouth instead of in his mouth! I definitely can do better than that. When my turn came up, I was very excited. I have never had peanut butter before, as my mom does not typically let me have any people food. The contest began and I was in heaven, eating all that yummy peanut butter. Next thing I knew it was over and I was tied for first place with a little wiener dog. What? That did not seem possible! So there was a run-off for first place with cream cheese instead of peanut butter (still pretty good to me!). The whistle blew and we were off. I quickly made the cream cheese on the spoon disappear, but alas, the judges said I lost by a single lick! I couldn't believe it, and I was so disappointed. I think that Mom was in shock, too! I would definitely like a rematch one day! - **Max**

Top Ten Dog Beaches

1. **Fisherman's Cove** – Manasquan, New Jersey
2. **Ft. DeSoto Paw Beach** – St. Petersburg, Florida

3. **Hendry's Beach** – Santa Barbara, California
4. **Dog Beach** – San Diego, California

5. **Gulfside Beach** – Sanibel, Florida
6. **Assateague National Seashore** – Ocean City, Maryland

7. **Oak Island** – Wilmington, North Carolina

8. **Bonita Beach** – Fort Myers, Florida

9. **Brohard Paw Park** – Venice, Florida
10. **Coronado Island** – San Diego, California

Chapter 7

Fun Facts

🐾 Petting dogs is proven to lower blood pressure in humans.

🐾 Dogs can be trained to detect sicknesses in people, such as cancer.

🐾 It is perfectly normal for a puppy to sleep up to 19 hours per day.

🐾 People with pets live longer, have less stress, and have fewer heart attacks.

🐾 Dogs and cats turn in circles before lying down because in the wild this instinctive action turns long grass into a bed.

🐾 The Doberman was created by a German tax collector in order to be his bodyguard.

🐾 The French Bulldog originated in England.

🐾 The Bedlington Terrier looks like a lamb

Kayla and her Kids

I have **never seen** anything like it in all my (short) years at the dog park. The park could be full of dogs running around in every direction, and the second a kid enters the park my friend, Kayla, is there waiting for them. I have even seen Kayla waiting at the gate for a child to enter. Kayla will bring the child a ball or Frisbee and put it at their feet, waiting for them to throw it, and they always do! From that moment on, it is just Kayla and her chosen child playing together. Sometimes it bothers me because I love to play with Kayla, but Kayla always prefers the kids.

I get it, though. They throw the ball for her and they run around and play chase with her. I do not do either of those things well. First of all, I can't throw a ball, and secondly, I am not a natural runner. I prefer to wrestle with other dogs, and unfortunately, Kayla doesn't like to wrestle. It is amazing to watch Kayla with the kids, though. The kids all love her, and she never gets tired of playing with them. While Kayla is very sweet with the kids, she does require them to throw toys for her non-stop, and they always do. In fact, the kids all look for Kayla the minute they enter the dog park. The parents love her, too. Not only are their dogs having fun at the dog park, but their kids are, too. Kayla is the perfect babysitter/play date. Her pet parent Tony has taught her well. – **Luther**

Neighborhood Devotion

One of my best friends is our neighbor, Chloe. Chloe is a beautiful black Standard Poodle with a high prancing tail (I love that fluffy tail!). She was the first dog I met when I came to live with my mom. We get along great. Sometimes I think Chloe believes *she is my mom.* She and I love to play chase, and I especially like to try to get her tail. There has been many a time that I have walked away from our play session with clumps of black fur hanging from my mouth.... I can't believe that she lets me get away with that! As we live in a condo complex, Chloe and I see each other at least once a day for our usual meet and greet session. Chloe is almost as fond of my mom as she is of me (but not quite). Chloe likes to hang out at the top of her stairs and stare across the parking lot at our door. This way she is always ready to come down and say hi when my door opens. If we go too long without seeing each other, she gets very worried. Chloe's mom told me that she circles our parking space, sniffs our car, and even comes to our door to see if we are around. Now that's devotion. I also share Chloe's obsession in that every time Mom and I go out I either climb Chloe's stairs or stare up at her patio. It is always nice when love is shared! -**Max**

Canine Good Citizen Test

Let's be honest here; when we hear the word *test*, don't we all get just a little bit nervous? Well, let me tell you about my Canine Good Citizen test. First of all, my Mom didn't even tell me what we were doing, just that we were going on a field trip. Field trips are always fun and usually Max is with us, but not on that day. We went to this place where there were a bunch of animals, not just dogs and cats. I saw my first llama! I have to admit I was a little scared, as they are really big! I was now completely confused. What is going on? Why are we at this place? I soon learned that I was being tested to become a therapy dog. Well, that sounds serious! I don't even know what a therapy dog does. Is it a spa for dogs?

As we entered the room, a very nice lady greeted us. She petted me, hugged me, pulled at my jowls, and tickled my feet. Cool! I decided to lie down so she could have easy access to my belly and give me a rub, which she did. So far, so good, I was having fun. Next, she made some loud noises and walked around me with some crutches and other noisy stuff. I couldn't figure out why she was doing that, so I just sat there and watched. No problem so far! The lady then made me walk around the room and pass up some dog treats. Yes, I was curious about the treats, but I was more interested in having her hug and pet me again. After I passed on the treats, she gave me a big hug and said I passed the test. Test? What test? I thought we were just playing! I don't know why Max is too afraid to even try out for this job. It is a piece of cake! I am going to love being a therapy dog! – **Luther**

Top Ten Dog-Related Careers

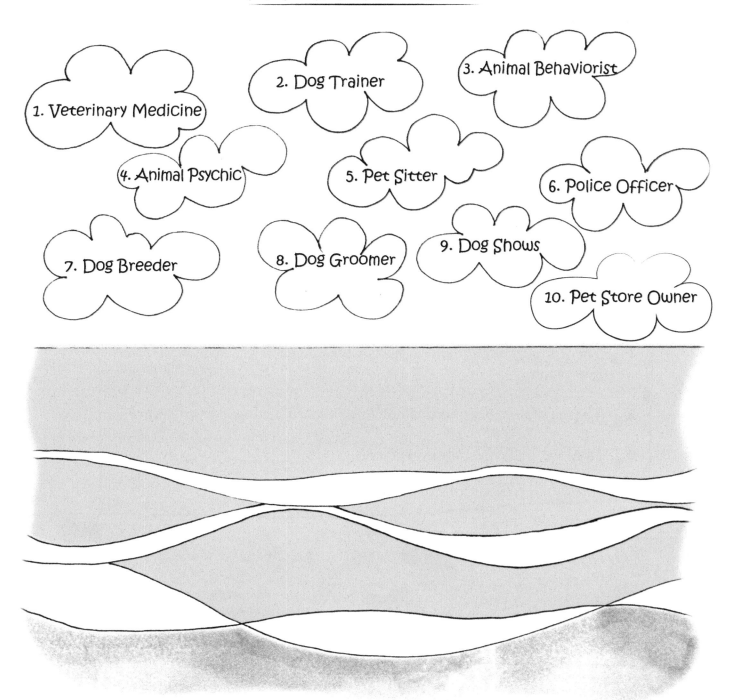

1. Veterinary Medicine
2. Dog Trainer
3. Animal Behaviorist
4. Animal Psychic
5. Pet Sitter
6. Police Officer
7. Dog Breeder
8. Dog Groomer
9. Dog Shows
10. Pet Store Owner

Chapter 8

Fun Facts

🐾 The Newfoundland has webbed feet like a duck.

🐾 The Irish Wolfhound is the tallest of the dog breeds.

🐾 Boxers are named for their habit of using their front paws for play.

🐾 The Bloodhound is the only animal whose evidence can be used in a courtroom.

🐾 A St. Bernard named Barry had the most rescues ever and saved 40 lives.

🐾 The Norwegian Lundehund has six toes on each foot, which helps him climb.

🐾 The Australian Shepherd is not Australian. The dog is from France.

🐾 Dogs eat both meat and vegetables.

Staircase Surprise

One night, Greta, a 190-pound Mastiff, was walking from her dog yard into her home when she took a wrong turn. She was an older dog, and her eyesight was not as good as it used to be. Greta missed the stairs and instead, she slid under them. To this day no one can figure out how she fit through that tiny space underneath the steps. Greta had slid butt-first and ended up stuck under the stairs and in the mud. Her mom did not know whether to laugh or cry. Here was this huge Mastiff stuck in a very muddy place! How was she going to get her out? I should also tell you that it was late at night and very dark out. Greta's mom climbed down into the tiny space (she barely fit) and tried to push Greta out, but had no luck. Greta weighed almost twice as much as her mom. Next, she called Greta's dad to come help, but he couldn't figure a way out for Greta either. Thankfully Greta was unfazed by her situation, and decided to take a nap in the mud while her parents figured out what to do. Finally, Greta's parents had to call the neighbors, who happened to be out to dinner, to come help. (They were very handy with tools, unlike Greta's parents) Their food had just been served, but they decided to take it to go and come rescue Greta from her sticky situation. They brought a bunch of tools to take apart the steps, and within minutes Greta walked out a free Mastiff. The great neighbors were treated to a spa day and dinner for their kindness. Thank goodness for great neighbors! I hope that never happens to me. -**Luther (Greta was my Mom's dog before me.)**

A Lazy Fergus

Fergus, a French Mastiff, was never known for being very active—or really being active at all! One day his mom decided that Fergus needed to get out of the house and go for a walk. So walk they did. What his parents failed to consider was the path they took. At the beginning of the walk it was all downhill, which of course meant that the walk home would be all uphill! This was not smart at all, and Fergus let them know what he thought about that. At the base of the last hill they had to climb, Fergus sat down and refused to budge. The house was in sight, but he refused to move another inch. He was done; no more exercise for him. His mom had to resort to flagging down passing cars and asking for a ride. I should tell you that they lived out in the country, where there were not too many cars. And may I also remind you that French Mastiffs are really big! Finally, after waiting a really long time, a nice man stopped and offered them a ride in his truck. He could not stop laughing because it took longer to load Fergus in the truck than the actual drive home. Fergus never had to leave his yard again. **-Luther**

Top Fifteen Dog Parks in the U.S.

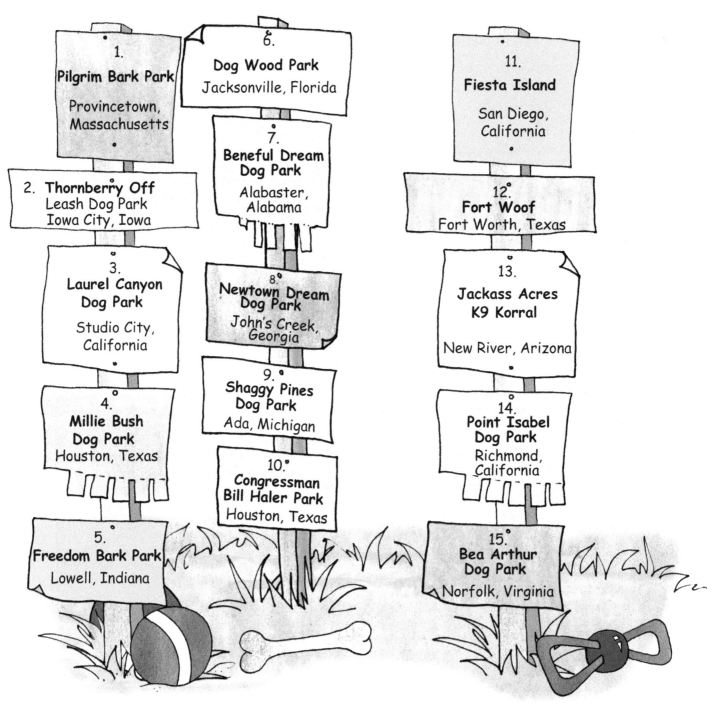

1. **Pilgrim Bark Park**
Provincetown,
Massachusetts

2. **Thornberry Off**
Leash Dog Park
Iowa City, Iowa

3. **Laurel Canyon
Dog Park**
Studio City,
California

4. **Millie Bush
Dog Park**
Houston, Texas

5. **Freedom Bark Park**
Lowell, Indiana

6. **Dog Wood Park**
Jacksonville, Florida

7. **Beneful Dream
Dog Park**
Alabaster,
Alabama

8. **Newtown Dream
Dog Park**
John's Creek,
Georgia

9. **Shaggy Pines
Dog Park**
Ada, Michigan

10. **Congressman
Bill Haler Park**
Houston, Texas

11. **Fiesta Island**
San Diego,
California

12. **Fort Woof**
Fort Worth, Texas

13. **Jackass Acres
K9 Korral**
New River, Arizona

14. **Point Isabel
Dog Park**
Richmond,
California

15. **Bea Arthur
Dog Park**
Norfolk, Virginia

Chapter 9

Fun Facts

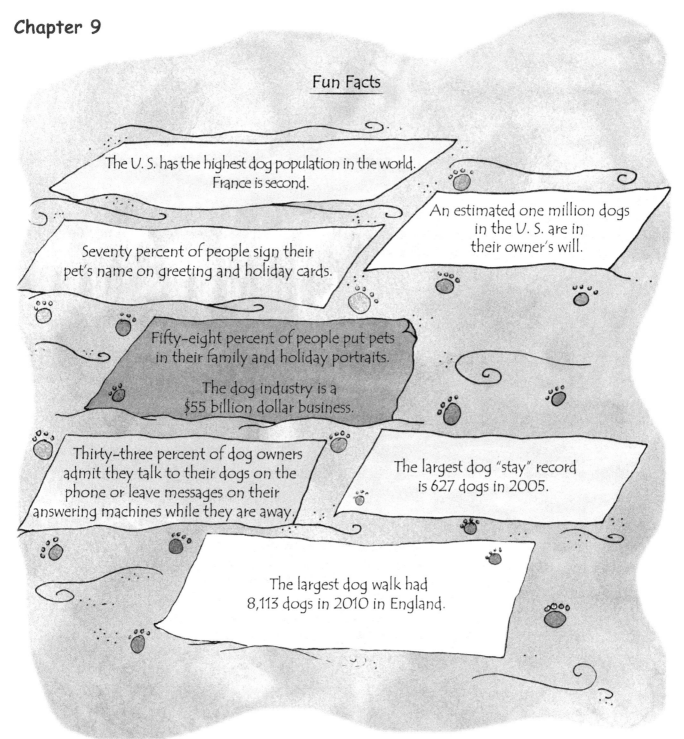

The U. S. has the highest dog population in the world. France is second.

An estimated one million dogs in the U. S. are in their owner's will.

Seventy percent of people sign their pet's name on greeting and holiday cards.

Fifty-eight percent of people put pets in their family and holiday portraits.

The dog industry is a $55 billion dollar business.

Thirty-three percent of dog owners admit they talk to their dogs on the phone or leave messages on their answering machines while they are away.

The largest dog "stay" record is 627 dogs in 2005.

The largest dog walk had 8,113 dogs in 2010 in England.

Loyal Protector

Mom's first dog was a large German Shepard named Baron. She was only a baby at the time and lived in a crib, which I think is kind of like my crate (I love my crate!). Baron immediately loved the baby (Mom) and followed her everywhere. He even started sleeping under her crib! Mom returned his affection. She loved to crawl after Baron and tried to ride him like a horse – I would never let a kid try that with me! They would often end up curled up on the floor taking a nap together. They were best buds.

One day Mom was crawling along and exploring the house with only Baron for company. On that day, the front door was left open (probably by her brother, Jimmy), and Mom thought it would be an excellent time to explore the great outdoors. Of course, what she did not know or understand was that the house was on a very busy street, with lots of cars driving by and was very dangerous. Mom started crawling down the sidewalk towards the street, unaware of the danger ahead. No one was around but Baron. Thankfully, Baron did not think this was a very good idea and decided to put an end to Mom's adventure. Baron grabbed onto Mom's diaper and started to drag her back into the house. Mom started to cry loudly! Quickly, the whole house came alive with activity. Baron was a hero and had saved the day! (Wow, that dog is going to be hard to live up to). This story proves to me just how valuable and loyal we dogs are. Treats and lots of love are always welcome as a thank you! - **Max**

Sprint for the Finish Line!

My mom and I participated in a 5k walk for charity with our friends, Kari and Max. This wasn't our first charity walk, and I thought my mom had learned from other walks that I am not cut out for three miles. Doesn't she realize how big I am? I can do two miles, maybe; but three is simply out of the question. I did not finish the walk, and decided about halfway through the walk that I'd had enough. Kari and Max, on the other hand, finished in style, barely breaking a sweat. I was passed out in the shade by the time they came across the finish line. This was not my best moment.

Where did I go wrong? you ask. Well, let me explain. I started the walk with gusto! I was dodging and weaving around walkers, trying to get to the front of the pack. Kari says it is my competitive nature, and I think she is right! I do not like having anyone in front of me. It did not take me long to get into the lead, with faithful Max by my side (he had to work to keep up with me!). Naturally, at this fast pace, we only stayed in front for about a mile. I am sure it was pretty funny watching a big Bulldog like me in the front of the pack! It was glorious while it lasted, but then I got tired. With two laps to go, I started to slow down like a toy losing its battery power. Max started to pull ahead of me and my mom, and the next thing I knew he and Kari were out of sight. Man, I was tired! My mom warned me that I needed to pace myself, but I assured her that this walk was a piece of cake. Remember that I am a stubborn Bulldog! It's hard for me to admit when I am wrong.

Mom was on it though, and knew exactly when to stop. We were able to double back to the start without anyone noticing. She spared me some embarrassment (I do have my pride, after all!).

Apparently we have a few more of these charity walks scheduled in the near future, and I am determined to finish them in style. Quitting is not an option. I have a lot of work to do if I want to cross the finish line with Max. Some people may say that I am a little competitive, but I prefer to call it *motivated*. Walkers, beware! - **Luther**

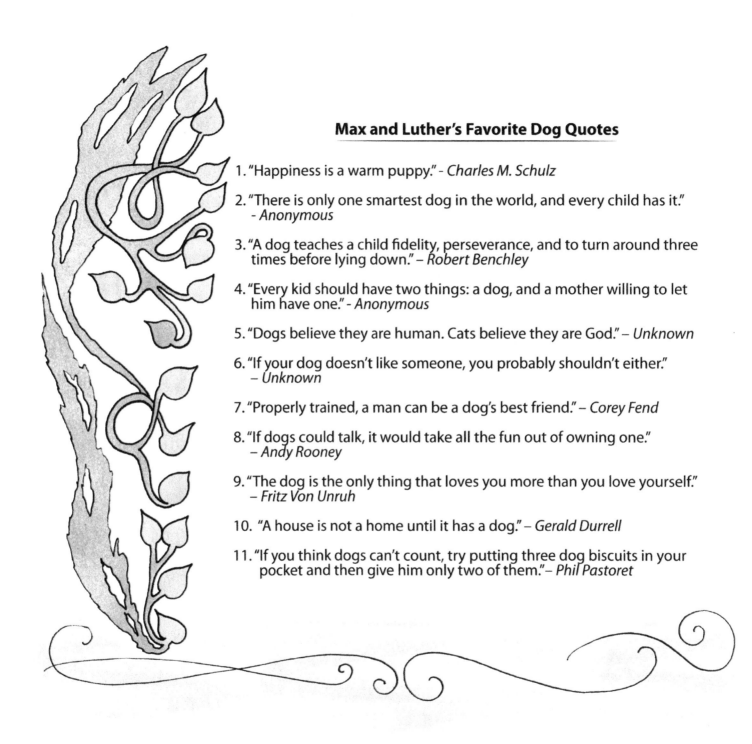

Max and Luther's Favorite Dog Quotes

1. "Happiness is a warm puppy." - *Charles M. Schulz*

2. "There is only one smartest dog in the world, and every child has it."
   - Anonymous

3. "A dog teaches a child fidelity, perseverance, and to turn around three times before lying down." – *Robert Benchley*

4. "Every kid should have two things: a dog, and a mother willing to let him have one." - *Anonymous*

5. "Dogs believe they are human. Cats believe they are God." – *Unknown*

6. "If your dog doesn't like someone, you probably shouldn't either."
   – *Unknown*

7. "Properly trained, a man can be a dog's best friend." – *Corey Fend*

8. "If dogs could talk, it would take all the fun out of owning one."
   – *Andy Rooney*

9. "The dog is the only thing that loves you more than you love yourself."
   – *Fritz Von Unruh*

10. "A house is not a home until it has a dog." – *Gerald Durrell*

11. "If you think dogs can't count, try putting three dog biscuits in your pocket and then give him only two of them."– *Phil Pastoret*

Chapter 10

Fun Facts

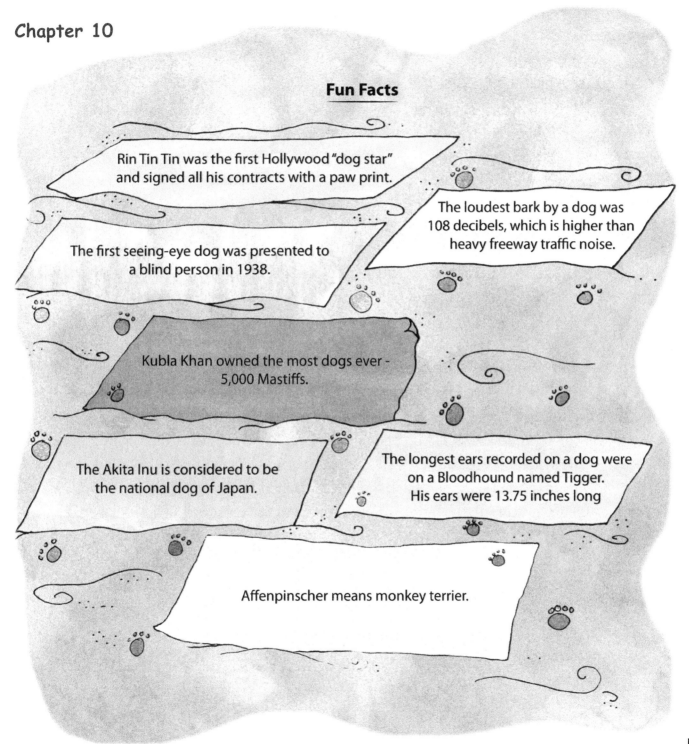

Rin Tin Tin was the first Hollywood "dog star" and signed all his contracts with a paw print.

The loudest bark by a dog was 108 decibels, which is higher than heavy freeway traffic noise.

The first seeing-eye dog was presented to a blind person in 1938.

Kubla Khan owned the most dogs ever - 5,000 Mastiffs.

The Akita Inu is considered to be the national dog of Japan.

The longest ears recorded on a dog were on a Bloodhound named Tigger. His ears were 13.75 inches long

Affenpinscher means monkey terrier.

Training Trials

As you may know, my dog mom was a Beagle. Beagles are well-known for being stubborn. I happen to think this is an excellent trait in a dog, but my mom does not agree. For the most part, training me to behave was a breeze. I will do anything for a treat! Who wouldn't? However, this is also my downfall. When I get that whiff of food in my nose, I have a hard time focusing on anything else. So Mom signed me up for lessons in the hope I could be trained to behave better off-leash. After a couple of months of training, my teacher said that this is as good as it gets, and for a Beagle I was pretty good! Was that supposed to be a compliment? Anyway, this gave my mom the confidence she needed to take me off-leash at the beach.

In our little beachside town, summers mean the beach is off limits to dogs. I really think that is not fair, but Mom says that tourists are our bread and butter (I am not sure what that actually means). Labor Day is when the beach opens up again to us dogs. It is the best day of the year! On our first day back to the beach, Mom and I had so much fun, running, splashing, and meeting new dogs! Freedom at last! Everything was perfect until I spied something interesting far down the beach and I took off. Mom yelled for me to stop, and I did. I looked back at her (she was still running after me) and I paused for a second. I then turned and kept on going. Hey, at least I thought about waiting for her. (See? The training did some good!) Mom eventually caught up with me, and that was the end of our beach day. I usually obey most of her commands (as she always carries treats for me when we are off-leash), but that day I was too excited...besides, I know we will be back next week! – **Max**

I Pee Freely

I recently met Mason at the dog park and boy, is he a wild one. He is a one-year-old Pointer, and did I mention that he is wild? He pees on everything in sight (and I mean everything!). It is incredible. I have never seen anything like it. He even pees on things as he runs and plays. I can't figure out how he can run, lift a leg, and pee on something without losing his balance. He really needs to enter a talent contest, because he would win hands down.

Mason's funniest move came when he peed on my mom. Mason casually walked up to her pretending he wanted to be petted, and as she was petting him, he lifted his leg and *Bam!* He peed on her knee, which dripped all the way down her leg. Mom was totally cool about it! She understood how puppies can be and totally laughed it off. As she was wearing flip-flops, it was easy to clean off in the water fountain. However, Mom did watch him closely after that so that there would be no more accidents. When he would come near her, she would quickly step out of "pee range." His owners are hoping that one day he will outgrow this habit. I am not so sure about that. He seems to be having too much fun to stop. I certainly hope I see him again. It is fun to watch him in action. Beware of Mason! - **Luther**

The Unfinished Walk

Mom told me about another dog she had growing up, Sassy the Scottish Terrier. What a dumb name for a dog! Mom's little sister named her when she was very young, which should serve as a cautionary tale to other dog owners. Sassy was a good dog, but not very active. Her favorite thing to do was to lay her snout across any human's leg she could find and nap. Sassy could do this for hours. Mom and her siblings tried to get Sassy to play and be more active, but she would have none of it. They would try to take her on walks around the block, but Sassy would only make it about halfway before she would sit down and refuse to move another inch. She always had to be carried home. Good thing she was a small dog! Mom would never let me get away with that. Our daily walks (which some people might call hikes) are at least 3 to 4 miles long, and Mom says I am much too big now to carry. In all her years of living, Sassy never completed a single walk. That is what I call having a dog's life! – **Max**

Ten Foods to Never Feed your Dog

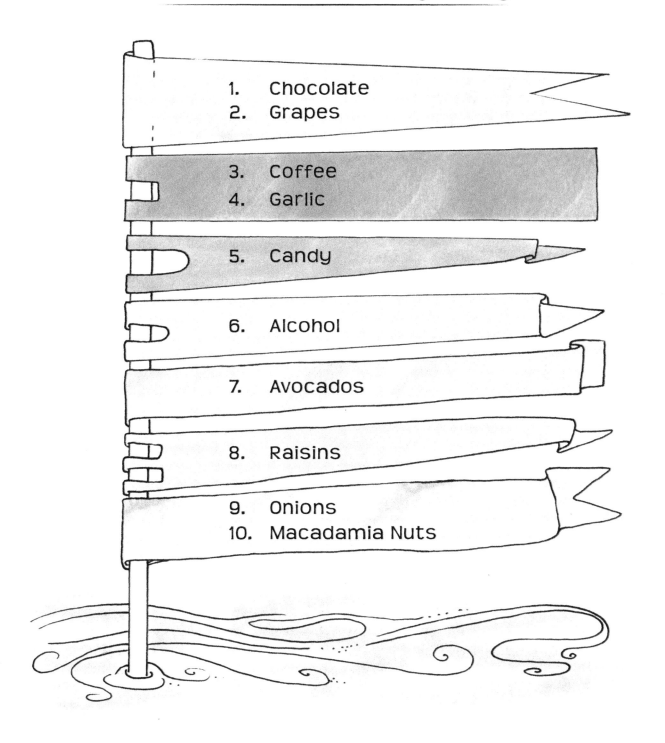

1. Chocolate
2. Grapes
3. Coffee
4. Garlic
5. Candy
6. Alcohol
7. Avocados
8. Raisins
9. Onions
10. Macadamia Nuts

"Life is not complete without a Dog."

Authors' Biography

Southern California residents, Kari Sherman and Carey Laubenberg met two years ago at the dog park when their two dogs, Max and Luther, became instant friends. They soon discovered they had much more in common than just their dogs. After constantly regaling each other with their funny stories and encounters at the dog park, dog beach, and other places, they decided that Max and Luther should share their stories with others and the "True Tails" series was born. Book I was published in October 2014 and Book III is planned for release in 2016.

Join Max and Luther on their continuing adventures:

Website: www.kariandcarey.com
Facebook: maxandlutherpublication
Instagram: maxandluther
Twitter: @dogparktails

CPSIA information can be obtained
at www.ICGtesting.com
Printed in the USA
LVOW05s1309260218
567892LV00031B/928/P